Upcycle Quilts

by Linda Causee

Leisure Arts, Inc.
Maumelle, Arkansas

Produced by

Production Team

Creative Directors:	Jean Leinhauser and Rita Weiss
Book Design:	Linda Causee
Technical Editor:	Ann Harnden

Diagrams © 2017 by The Creative Partners LLC

Reproduced by special permission.

We have made every effort to ensure that these instructions are accurate and complete. We cannot, however, be responsible for human error, typographical mistakes or variations in individual work.

Published by Leisure Arts, Inc.

the art of everyday living

Library of Congress Control Number: 2016942651

ISBN-13: 978-1-4647-5233-9

Introduction

"Upcycle" is a new word I've just recently added to my dictionary. It means "creative reuse": a way of changing waste materials or unwanted products into a new product that will be better for the environment.

An "Upcycle Quilt" is just that. It's a quilt created from unwanted materials that you no longer want or need but just couldn't throw away, such as Grandma's handkerchiefs or Dad's shirts.

What do you do with all those socks that used to be pairs, but now somehow there is only one? Just throw out the remaining sock, or put it to work to create a clever quilt?

What about all those sweaters that no longer fit anyone and are certainly too worn to give away? Why not continue to keep someone warm by putting those old sweaters to work together in a quilt?

Have a drawer filled with the clothes that one of your favorite children—now almost ready for college—wore when he was a baby? Do you keep all of your grandmother's doilies but never use them? Upcycle them!

If you only have a few "no longer wanteds," make a simple wall hanging. But if your closets are stuffed with "leftovers" and "has beens," why not make a full-size quilt. Whichever size you choose to make, you will be creating that Upcycle product that will not only be better for the environment but will add beauty to your home.

And if you've never made a quilt before, or if you're not sure of your quilting ability, we've included some basic instructions you'll need not just as a quilter but a quilter who knows how to help the environment by Upcycling.

Contents

Baby Memories   6

Dad's Shirts   12

Hanky Parade   16

Sweater Throw Quilt   20

Beach Blanket   23

Fit for a King   26

Spiritual Solace   30

Sock Crazy   33

Red, White, and Blue   40

Totes Galore   43

General Directions   46

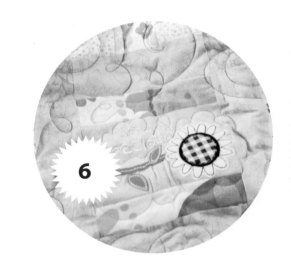

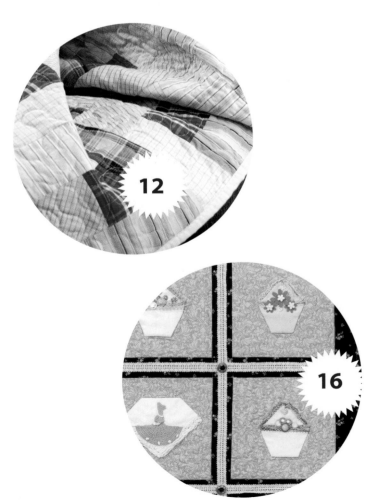

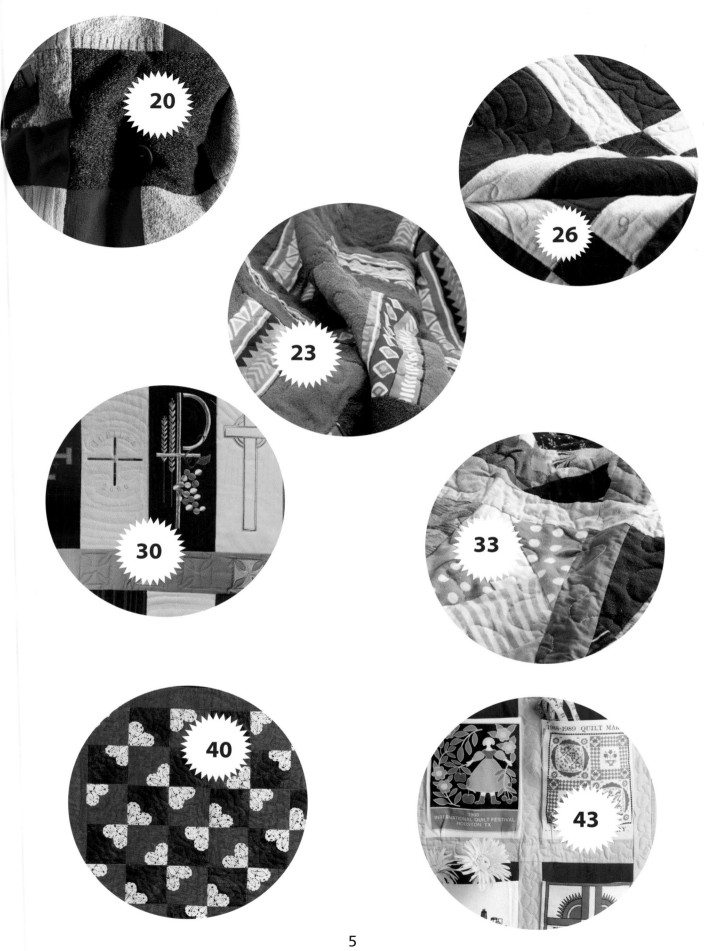

Baby Memories

Approximate Size: 56" x 72"

Those outfits that baby once wore can now be part of a wonderful quilt.

Materials

- 10-12 assorted baby clothes
- 2 yds pink tone-on-tone fabric
- 1 yd turquoise tone-on-tone fabric
- 1 yd lavender tone-on-tone fabric
- 1¼ yds stripe fabric
- 3½ yds backing fabric
- batting

Cutting

Note: *The following cutting instructions use the baby clothes to the best advantage. Depending on your collection (size and shape), you may choose to make different amounts of each block.*

Note: *Read Tips for Working with Baby Clothes, page 8, before cutting.*

Block 1 - Nine Patch (5 blocks)

45 squares, 2½" x 2½", assorted baby clothes

Block 2 - Four Patch (2 blocks)

8 squares, 3½" x 3½", assorted baby clothes

Block 3 - Stripes (18 blocks)

54 strips, 3½" x 6½", assorted baby clothes

Block 4 - Picture Frame (1 block)

1 square, 4½" x 4½", baby clothes

2 strips, 1½" x 4½", baby clothes

2 strips, 1½" x 6½", baby clothes

Block 5 - "Drunkard's Path" (4 blocks)

4 squares, 6½" x 6½", pink fabric

4 strips, 6½" long, ruffle baby clothes (ruffle is about 2½" wide)

Block 6 - Plain Square (5 blocks)

5 squares, 6½" x 6½", assorted baby clothes

Finishing

58 strips, 2½" x 6½", pink fabric (sashing)

24 squares, 2½" x 2½", turquoise fabric (corner squares)

7 strips, 2½"x width of fabric, pink fabric (first border)

7 strips, 3½"x width of fabric, lavender fabric (second border)

8 strips, 4½"x width of fabric, stripe fabric (third border)

8 strips, 2½"x width of fabric, turquoise fabric (binding)

continued on page 8

Tips for Working with Baby Clothes

- Sort baby clothes in groups of similar types and colors. The clothes used in the photographed quilt are mainly soft single knit items.

- Use **thin** fusible interfacing on wrong side of knit clothes for easier handling and sewing since they will be somewhat stretchy.

- If using fabrics that are different thicknesses, use **medium** fusible interfacing on the thinner fabrics.

- Cut off sleeves, then cut front from back at shoulder and side seams. **Note:** *Cut along each side close to seam.*

- For **Nine Patch blocks**, you will need 9 squares, 5 of one fabric and 4 of another.

- For **Four Patch blocks**, you will need 4 squares, 2 of one fabric and 2 of another.

- For the **Stripes blocks**, you will need 3 strips, 2 of one fabric and 1 of another.

- For the **Picture Frame block**, fussy cut a square to show off a favorite motif. Then use strips from another fabric for the frame.

- For the **"Drunkard's Patch" block**, use a ruffle from a dress or hat to form the curve of the block.

- For the **Plain Squares**, you can showcase a favorite motif or appliqué by fussy cutting around it.

Fussy Cutting

Use your acrylic ruler and place on top of the fabric, centering the motif. Cut the fabric to the size needed, being sure to add seam allowance along each edge.

Instructions

Block 1 - Nine Patch

1. For rows 1 and 3, sew three 2½" x 2½" squares together. Press seams in one direction.

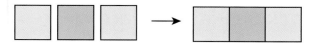

2. For row 2, sew three contrasting 2½" x 2½" squares together. Press seams in opposite direction.

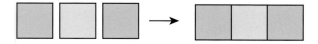

3. Sew rows 1, 2 and 3 together to complete Block 1 - Nine Patch. The photographed quilt has a total of five Nine-Patch blocks.

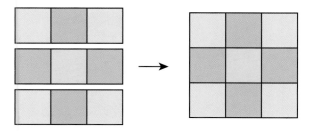

Block 2 - Four Patch

1. Sew two 3½" x 3½" contrasting squares together; press seam toward darker fabric. Repeat.

2. Sew pairs of squares together to complete Four Patch. Photographed quilt has a total of two Four Patch blocks.

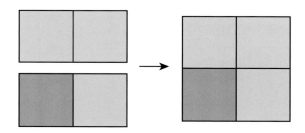

Block 3 - Stripes

1. Sew three 2½" x 6½" strips together to complete Stripes block. The photographed quilt has 18 Stripes blocks.

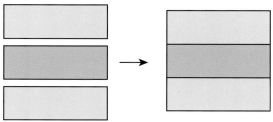

9

continued on page 10

Block 4 - Picture Frame Block

1. Sew a 1½" x 4½" strip to each side of a 4½" x 4½" square. Press seams toward strips.

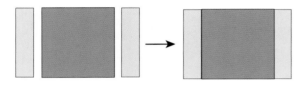

2. Sew a 1½" x 6½" strip to top and bottom. Press seams toward strips to complete block. The photographed quilt has one Picture Frame block.

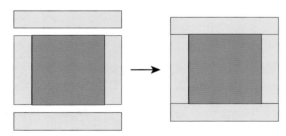

Block 5 - "Drunkard's Path" Block

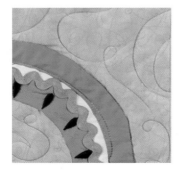

1. Position the left short edge of 6½"-long ruffle, about 2½" from lower left corner of

pink 6½" x 6½" square; pin in place. Position right short edge of ruffle along adjacent edge. Pin ruffle in place in a nice curve.

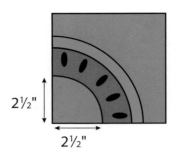

Note: *If there are raw edges, fold under and pin in place.*

2. Hand or machine sew both curved edges in place. The photographed quilt has four Drunkard's Path blocks.

Block 6 - Plain Square

Showcase a motif, an overall design or section of clothing for the 6½" x 6½" Plain Squares. The photographed quilt has five Plain Squares.

Finishing your Quilt

1. Referring to Quilt Layout and photograph, place blocks in seven rows of five blocks with 2½" x 6½" pink sashing strips and 2½" x 2½" turquoise squares in between.

2. For block rows, sew blocks with 2½" x 6½" pink sashing strips in between.

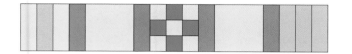

3. For sashing rows, sew 2½" x 6½" pink sashing strips with 2½" x 2½" turquoise squares in between.

4. Sew block and sashing rows together.

5. Referring to Adding Borders, page 57, attach 2½"-wide pink border to sides first then to top and bottom.

6. Repeat step 5 with 3½"-wide lavender border and 4½"-wide striped border.

7. Refer to Finishing Your Quilt, pages 60 to 64, to complete your quilt.

Quilt Layout

Dad's Shirts

Approximate Size 45" x 60"

Dad may no longer be wearing these shirts to go off to the office, but cut up and put together, they become a great Log Cabin quilt and a perfect reminder of Dad.

Materials

6-8 shirts (depending on shirt size)

2¾ yds backing fabric

½ yd binding fabric

batting

Cutting

Blocks

48 squares, 3" x 3", red shirts

48 squares, 3" x 3", assorted plaid shirts

96 rectangles, 3" x 5½", assorted plaid shirts

48 rectangles, 3" x 8", assorted plaid shirts

Finishing

6 strips, 2½"-wide, binding fabric

Tips for Working with Clothing

• Try to use items that are similar in type and thickness.

• If some fabrics are thinner or more stretchy than others, use fusible interfacing to stabilize the fabric.

• Use a common shirt fabric for the center square 1.

• For square 2 and rectangles 3, 4, and 5, use random shirt fabrics for a scrappy look.

continued on page 14

Instructions

Blocks

Note: *The Log Cabin blocks can be made using the Foundation Piecing method, pages 50 to 57, and the pattern on the facing page. If you do not want to use a foundation, sew block using the following steps.*

1. Sew a 3" x 3" red square to a 3" x 3" plaid square. Press seam toward plaid square.

2. Turn squares clockwise and sew to a 3" x 5½" plaid rectangle. Press seam toward rectangle just added.

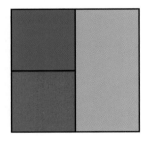

3. Turn unit just made counterclockwise and sew to another 3" x 5½" plaid rectangle. Press seam toward rectangle just added.

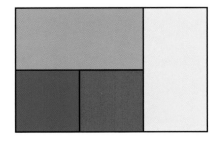

4. Turn unit counterclockwise again and sew to a 3" x 8" plaid rectangle. Press seam toward rectangle just added. Make a total of 48 Log Cabin blocks.

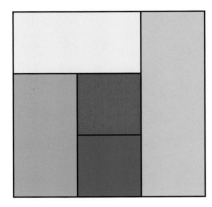

Finishing

1. Referring to Quilt Layout and photo, place blocks in eight rows of six blocks.

2. Sew blocks together in rows; then sew rows together.

3. Refer to Finishing Your Quilt, pages 60 to 64, to complete your quilt.

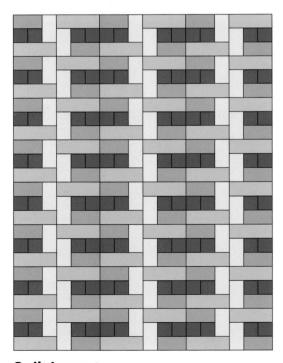

Quilt Layout

14

Note: *Add ¼" seam allowance to each outside edge when cutting pattern.*

Hanky Parade
Approximate Size 39" x 39"

You have some of Grandma's hankies that you don't want to use,
but you don't want them to just sit in a drawer. So what better answer could
there be than to show them off in a quilt!

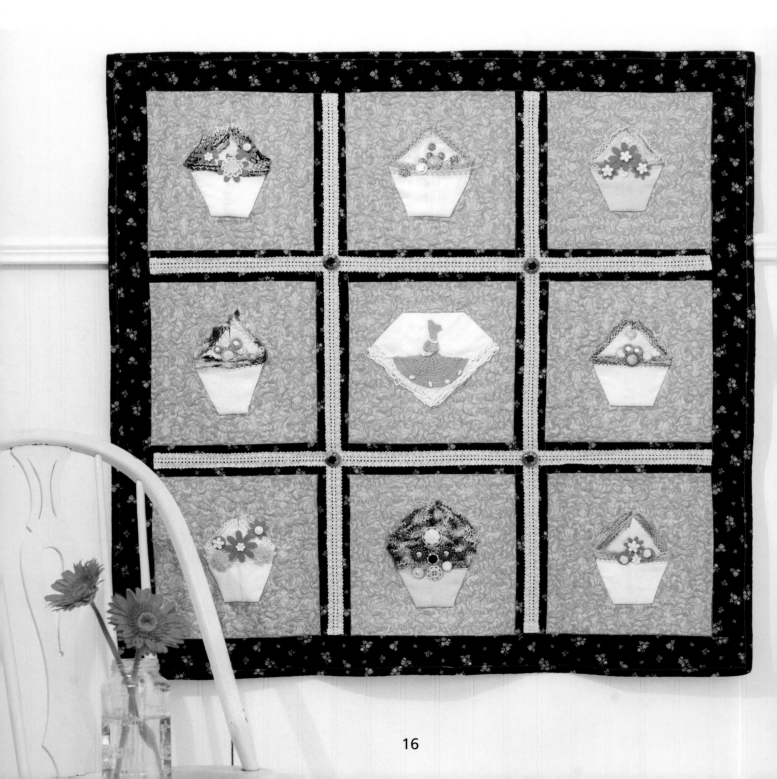

Materials

9 assorted lace hankies

1 yd pink print

1 yd black/pink print

4 yards 1"-wide flat lace

1½ yds backing fabric

thin cotton batting

assorted novelty buttons

Cutting

9 squares, 10½" x 10½", pink print

6 strips, 2½" x 10½", black/pink print (sashing)

2 strips, 2½" x 34½", black/pink print (sashing)

2 strips, 3" x 34½", black/pink print (border)

2 strips, 3" x 38½", black/pink print (border)

4 strips, 34½" long, 1"-wide flat lace

4 strips, 2½"x width of fabric, black/pink print

Tips for Working with Hankies

• Decide how you would like to showcase your hankies. If they are lace-edged, you probably will not want to cut them. So, as in the photograph, you can fold them so that all the lace shows and attach them to a background square.

• Fold hankies to form little baskets. See page 18.

• Showcase a corner motif, such as the Sunbonnet Sue in the center of the photographed quilt.

• You can also use the hankies flat on a fabric square.

17

continued on page 18

Instructions

Preparing the Hanky Baskets

1. To make hanky basket, open hanky and place wrong side up on a flat surface.

2. Fold hanky in half with wrong sides together.

3. Fold lower right corner up towards center.

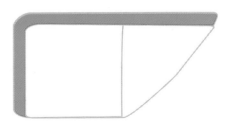

4. Fold lower left corner up towards center.

5. Fold left side up toward center.

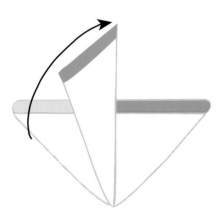

6. Fold right side up in same manner toward center.

7. Fold lower point up as shown.

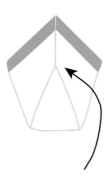

8. Turn hanky over for finished basket.

Making the Blocks

1. Center the hanky basket on the right side of a 10½" x 10½" pink print square; pin in place.

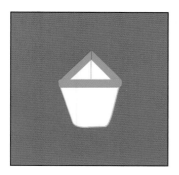

2. Tack in place by hand with sewing needle and matching thread or by machine. Make a total of 9 hanky basket blocks.

Note: *The photographed quilt is made with a hanky trimmed with a Sunbonnet Sue corner rather than a basket block.*

Sewing the Quilt

1. Place the hanky blocks in a pleasing arrangement.

2. Sew the blocks together in rows with 2½" x 10½" black/pink print sashing strips in between.

3. Sew the rows together with 2½" x 34½" black/pink print sashing strips in between.

4. Referring to photo and Quilt Layout, place 34½"-long strips of flat lace centered on sashing strips; tack in place by hand or machine.

5. Sew a 3" x 34½" black/pink print strip to each side of quilt. Sew a 3" x 39½"black/pink print strip to the top and bottom of the quilt.

6. Refer to Finishing Your Quilt, pages 60 to 64, to complete your quilt.

7. Referring to photograph on page 16, sew a button where lace strips cross. Sew buttons in clusters on hanky baskets.

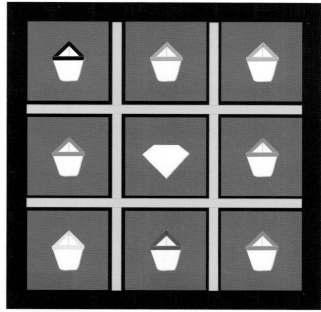

Quilt Layout

Sweater Throw Quilt

Approximate Size: 45" x 65"

Do you have drawers full of old sweaters that no one wears any longer, but you can't bear to throw them away. If so, make a "Sweater Throw" Quilt to snuggle under on a cold winter's night.

Materials

10-12 assorted adult-sized sweaters

6-8 yds fusible interfacing

2 yds fleece for backing

12 assorted large buttons

Cutting

Note: *Read Tips for Working with Sweaters below before cutting.*

32 rectangles, 8½" x 7½", assorted sweaters

7 rectangles, 16" x 14", assorted sweaters

Tips for Working with Sweaters

• Use sweaters with similar thickness for your quilt.

• Cut off sleeves from sweater; then cut sleeves at seams. Next, cut front from back at side and shoulder seams.

• Following manufacturer's directions, iron fusible interfacing to wrong side of front, back and sleeves (if large enough to use).

• Decide which sweaters you will use for the Four-Patch blocks. Be sure that they are contrasting in color. You will need two patches each of two contrasting rectangles.

Note: *The size of your blocks will depend on the size of the sweaters being used. Find the smallest sweater and cut the largest square possible. Then cut the same-sized squares/ rectangles from remaining sweaters.*

continued on page 22

Instructions

Note: *Read Tips for Working with Sweaters, page 21, before beginning.*

Making the Four-Patch Blocks

1. Place the 8½" x 7½" rectangles in pairs. Decide which pairs will make up your Four-Patch blocks. You will need a total of eight Four-Patch blocks.

2. Sew a pair of rectangles together using a ½" seam allowance. Repeat.

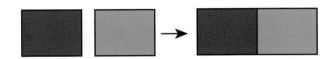

3. Sew pairs together to complete Four-Patch block. Repeat for remaining blocks.

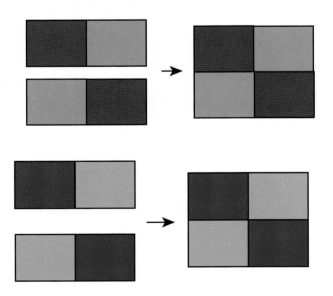

Making the Quilt

1. Referring to photo and Quilt Layout, place Four-Patch blocks and 16" x 14" rectangles in five rows of three.

2. Sew blocks together in rows; then sew rows together using a ½" seam allowance.

3. Place sweater quilt top right side up on fleece backing. Be sure that fleece extends 2" beyond each edge of quilt top.

4. Quilt as desired.

5. Trim fleece 1" from edge of quilt top.

6. Turning under raw edge, fold fleece over edge of quilt top; machine stitch along edge of fleece to form "mock" binding. **Hint:** *Use a zigzag stitch or your favorite embroidery stitch.*

7. Sew two buttons down the center of each large rectangle.

Quilt Layout

Beach Blanket

Approximate Size: 48" x 60"

You are ready to update your bathroom and need to get new bath towels. But, what can you do with the old towels that may be in perfectly good condition? Make a quilt that you can take to the beach or a picnic, of course!

Materials

Assorted large bath towels

> **Note**: *Photographed quilt uses 1 turquoise, 1 purple, 1 fuschia, 1 orange and 2 print towels.*

3 yds backing fabric

½ yd binding

Cutting

Blocks

12 strips, 5" x 13", orange

12 strips, 5" x 13", fuschia

12 strips, 5" x 13", turquoise

12 strips, 5" x 13", purple

24 strips, 5" x 13", print

Finishing

7 strips, 3"-wide, binding

Working with Towels

Note: *Towels can vary in size; therefore you may need more than 5 towels to complete your beach blanket.*

Towels are made from terry cloth which is a thick, absorbent fabric that has certain challenges when working with it:

- Terry cloth is very messy to work with. It sheds a great deal when cut. So you will need to clean your work area and sewing machine often.

- Since terry cloth is thick, you need to use a longer stitch length and a heavy-duty sewing needle.

Instructions

Making the Blocks

Note: *Use a ½" seam allowance.*

1. Sew an orange strip to opposite sides of a print strip to complete block. Repeat for a total of 6 orange blocks.

2. Sew a fuschia strip to opposite sides of a print strip to complete block. Repeat for a total of 6 fuschia blocks.

3. Sew a turquoise strip to opposite sides of a print strip to complete block. Repeat for a total of 6 turquoise blocks.

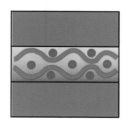

4. Sew a purple strip to opposite sides of a print strip to complete block. Repeat for a total of 6 purple blocks.

Making the Quilt

1. Referring to Quilt Layout, place blocks in six rows of four blocks. Sew together in rows, then sew rows together.

2. Place quilt top wrong sides together with backing fabric. **Note:** *Batting is not necessary due to thickness of the towels.* Quilt as desired.

3. Refer to Finishing Your Quilt, pages 60 to 64, to add binding.

Quilt Layout

Fit for a King

Approximate Size: 65" x 87"

Those drawstring bags that held the favorite beverages of the men in the family could now make a great quilt !

Materials

35 flannel drawstring gift bags

4½ yds purple flannel

2 yds gold flannel

4 yds fleece for backing

Cutting

Blocks

*35 rectangles, flannel bags

*70 strips, 3½" x 5½", purple flannel

*70 strips, 2½" x 9½", purple flannel

*If your bags are different sizes, you may have to adjust the sizes of your rectangles and strips. See Instructions, page 28.

Finishing

58 strips, 2½" x 9 ½", gold flannel

30 squares, 2½" x 2½", purple flannel

8 strips, 2½"-wide, gold flannel (first border)

9 strips, 4½"-wide, purple flannel (second border)

9 strips, 2½"-wide, purple flannel (binding)

Working with Flannel Fabric Bags

• Many silver bowls and cups, bottles of liquor or perfume, and jewelry are packaged in flannel bags; therefore, they can come in a variety of sizes.

• Flannel is rough on needles, so be sure to use a fresh needle when starting your project.

• Flannel has a loose weave; therefore a lot of lint can be produced while sewing. Be sure to clean the bobbin case and area around the bobbin and needle shaft during and after finishing your project.

• Because of the loose weave of flannel, it can shift and stretch a little while sewing. Use a walking foot to prevent shifting.

• Spray the wrong side of flannel with spray starch to stabilize the fabric. Be sure to let the fabric dry completely before sewing.

continued on page 28

Instructions

Note: *The flannel bags in the photographed quilt were three different sizes, resulting in three different sizes for the centers:*

    A. 3½" x 3½"

    B. 3½" x 5½"

    C. 3½" x 7½"

Depending on the size of the center, the sizes of side strips and the top and bottom strips will be different. Refer to the block diagrams below for cut sizes for the three different block center sizes.

You will need a total of 35 blocks for this quilt.

Blocks

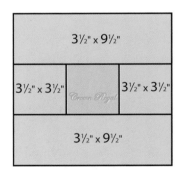

A. Block Center
3½" x 3½"

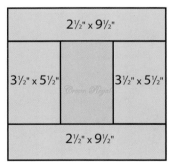

B. Block Center
3½" x 5½"

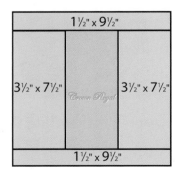

A. Block Center
3½" x 7½"

1. For Block A, sew a 3½" x 3½" purple square to opposite sides of a 3½" x 3½" center square. Press seams away from center.

2. Sew a 3½" x 9½" purple strip to the top and bottom. Press seams away from center.

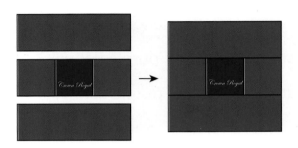

3. Repeat steps 1 and 2 for Block B (with a 3½" x 5½" center), using 3½" x 5½" strips for the sides and 2½" x 9½" for the tops and bottoms.

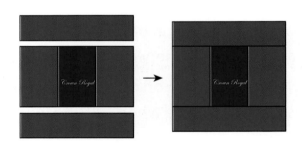

4. Repeat steps 1 and 2 for Block C (with a 3½" x 7½" center), using 3½" x 7½" strips for the sides and 1½" x 9½" for the tops and bottoms.

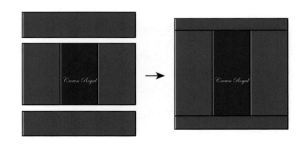

Finishing your Quilt

1. Referring to Quilt Layout and photo, place blocks in seven rows of five blocks.

2. For block rows, sew blocks together in rows with 2½" x 9½" gold strips in between. You will have seven block rows.

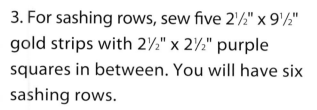

3. For sashing rows, sew five 2½" x 9½" gold strips with 2½" x 2½" purple squares in between. You will have six sashing rows.

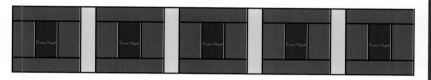

4. Sew block rows and sashing rows together.

5. Refer to Adding Borders, page 57, to sew 2½"-wide gold strips to sides of quilt top, then to top and bottom.

6. Repeat step 5 for second border to sew 4½"-wide purple strips to sides of quilt top and then to top and bottom.

7. Refer to Finishing Your Quilt, pages 60 to 64, to complete your quilt.

Quilt Layout

Spiritual Solace

Approximate Size: 28" x 39½"

Warm the room with a beautiful collection of elegant crosses.

Materials

8-9 assorted elegant fabrics

⅝ yd green satin charmeuse

½ yd gold brocade (binding)

1 yd backing fabric

thin batting

Cutting

8 rectangles, 6" x 15½", assorted elegant fabrics

1 strip, 4" x 22½", green satin charmeuse (sashing strip)

2 strips, 3½" x 34", green satin charmeuse (side border)

2 strips, 3½" x 28½", green satin charmeuse (top and bottom border)

4 strips, 2½"-wide, gold brocade (binding)

Tips for Working with Elegant and Embroidered Fabrics

• Handle elegant fabrics carefully. Some may fray more than others.

• If you don't have elegant fabric, you can still make this wall hanging using clothing or other items that have appliqués.

continued on page 32

Instructions

Finishing

1. Referring to Quilt Layout and photo, place 6" x 15½" rectangles in two rows of four rectangles with 4" x 22½" sashing strip in between.

2. Sew four rectangles together, then sew remaining four rectangles together.

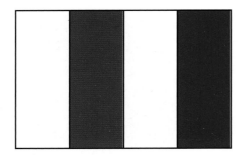

3. Sew rectangles to opposite sides of the sashing strip.

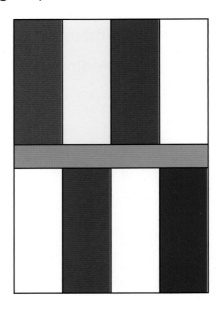

4. Referring to Adding Simple Borders, page 57, sew 3½" x 34" green strips to sides of quilt and 3½" x 28½" green strips to top and bottom.

5. Refer to Finishing Your Quilt, pages 60 to 64, to complete your quilt.

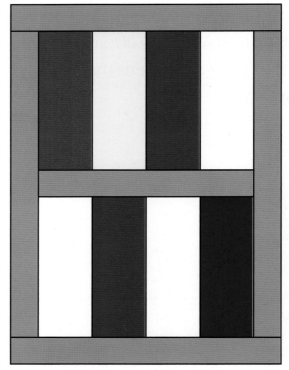

Quilt Layout

Sock Crazy

Approximate Size: 47½" x 47½"

Does your sock drawer contain lots of single socks whose mates have disappeared? Don't be concerned. Just turn those socks into an original quilt.

Materials

See Preparing the Foundation, page 51.

At least 2 dozen assorted socks (if you don't have enough socks, use scraps of fabric from your stash.)

1 yard muslin (optional)

½ yd pink print

½ yd blue print

¼ yd lavender print

1¼ yds bright print

2⅞ yds backing

batting

Optional: *2 yds lightweight fusible interfacing*

Patterns

Note: *Use patterns on pages 37 to 39 to make your foundations.*

Make 1 each of Patterns A to I

Cutting

Blocks

Note: *See Cutting the Fabric, page 51.*

9 squares, 11" x 11", muslin (optional)

Finishing

12 strips, 2½" x 11", pink print (sashings)

12 strips, 2½" x 11", blue print (sashings)

16 squares, 2½" x 2½", lavender print

5 strips, 4½"-wide, bright print (borders)

5 strips, 2½"-wide, bright print (binding)

Tips for Working with Socks

• Socks are stretchy, so you may want to use a lightweight fusible interfacing on the wrong side.

• Leave the heels attached for added interest in your blocks.

• Attach socks to a muslin foundation to give stability to the blocks. Use a blank muslin square and attach pieces randomly or use the patterns on pages 37 to 39.

• A paper foundation can also be used. It will need to be removed after completing quilt top.

Instructions

Making the Blocks

1. Cut toe off sock.

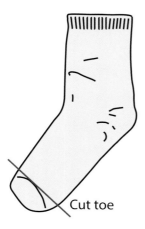

2. Cut off top band.

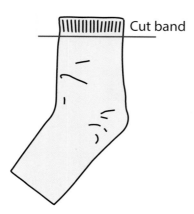

Cut band

2. Cut from open end to opposite open end down length of sock.

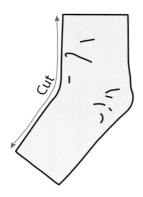

Cut

3. Open to have a flat piece.

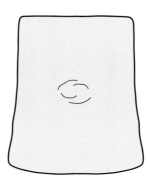

4. Repeat steps 1, 2 and 3 for each sock.

5. Referring to manufacturer's directions, fuse lightweight fusible interfacing to wrong side of cut socks.

6. Refer to Making the Blocks, pages 52 to 55, to make one block of each of the 9 block patterns.

Finishing Your Quilt

1. Referring to Quilt Layout, place blocks in three rows of three blocks with sashing and squares in between.

Quilt Layout

35

continued on page 36

2. Sew blocks and blue sashing strips together.

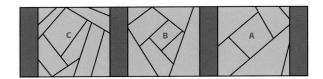

3. Sew pink sashing and lavender squares together.

4. Sew block and sashing rows together.

5. Refer to Adding Borders, page 57, to add 4½"-wide bright print border.

6. Refer to Finishing Your Quilt, pages 60 to 64, to complete your quilt.

Patterns

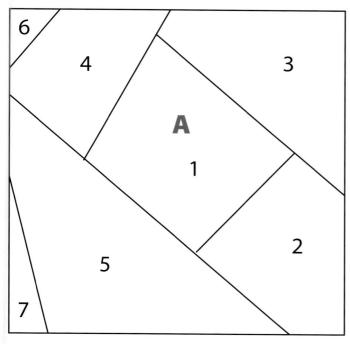

Enlarge All Patterns 300%

Notes: *Since Patterns A to I need to be 10½" x 10½" square for this quilt, you will need to make a copy of each pattern, enlarging them 300%. You can use your home copier or take them to your local office supply and copy store.*

Refer to Preparing the Foundation, page 51, to transfer the pattern onto your chosen foundation material.

Add ¼" seam allowance to each outside edge when cutting pattern.

Remember that the blocks will be mirror images of the patterns.

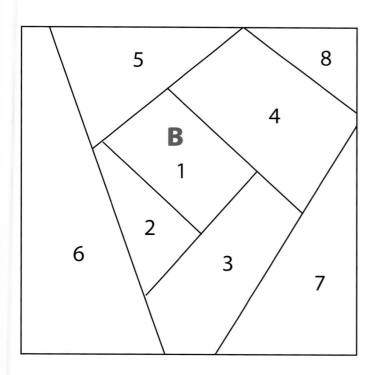

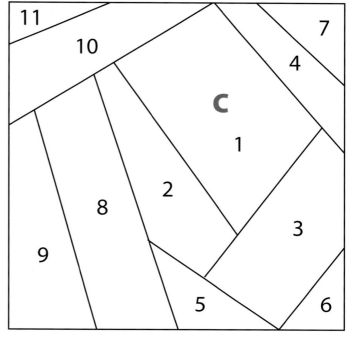

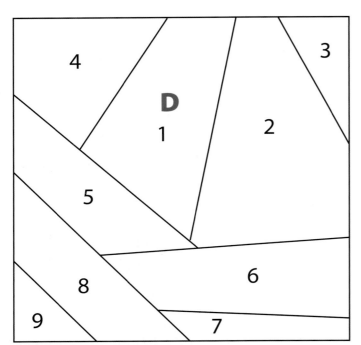

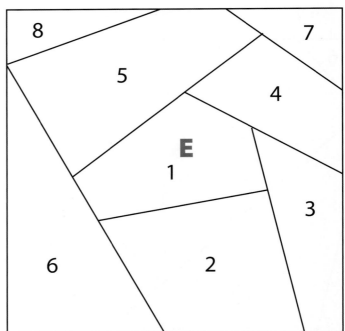

Enlarge All Patterns 300%

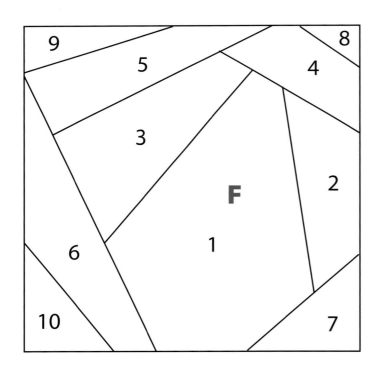

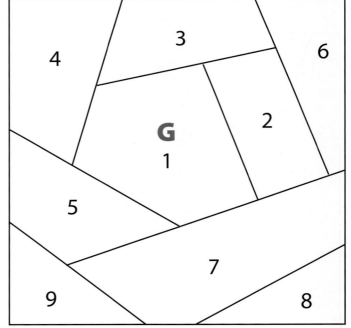

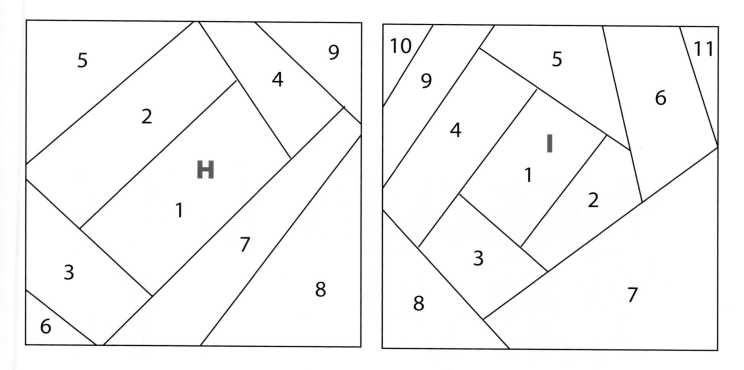

Enlarge All Patterns 300%

Red, White, and Blue

Approximate Size: 26" x 32"

A great use for the doilies that Grandma made, this quilt hanging on the wall shows a love for the colors of the flag—and Grandma's work.

Materials

12 round doilies (about 4" dia.)

1 yd red print

1 yd blue print

1 yd backing fabric

thin batting

Cutting

Blocks

24 squares, 3½" x 3½", red print

24 squares, 3½" x 3½", blue print

Finishing

2 strips, 2" x 24½", red print

2 strips, 2" x 21½", red print

2 strips, 3" x 27½", blue print

2 strips, 3" x 26½", blue print

2 strips, 2½"-wide, blue print (binding)

Working with Doilies

• The blocks in this quilt are a simplified version of a Drunkard's Path block. Instead of sewing curved edges together, you will tack a doily to a background square.

• Your blocks can be as large or small as dictated by the size of your doilies. The doilies used for the photographed quilt are about 4" diameter. If cut in quarters, the pieces will be about 2" x 2". The background square should be at least 1" to 1½" larger. The squares for this quilt are cut 3½" x 3½".

41

continued on page 42

Instructions

Making the Blocks

1. Cut all doilies carefully in quarters.

2. Place a quarter doily on the right side of a 3½" x 3½" square with straight edges along corner of block. Tack curved edge of doily to background square by hand or machine. Repeat for all 24 blue squares and 24 red squares.

3. Sew a blue and red square together; press seam toward blue; repeat.

4. Sew pairs of blocks together. Repeat for 12 blocks.

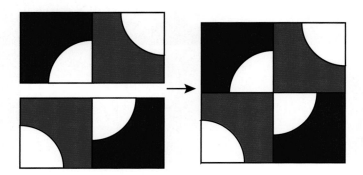

Finishing Your Quilt

1. Referring to Quilt Layout, place blocks together in 4 rows of 3 blocks. Sew blocks together in rows, then sew rows together.

2. Sew a 2" x 24½" red print strip to opposite sides of quilt; press seams toward border.

3. Sew a 2" x 21½" red print strip to top and bottom; press seams toward border.

4. Sew a 3" x 27½" blue print strip to opposite sides of quilt; press seams toward border.

5. Sew a 3" x 26½" blue print strip to top and bottom; press seams toward border.

6. Refer to Finishing Your Quilt, pages 60 to 64, to complete your quilt.

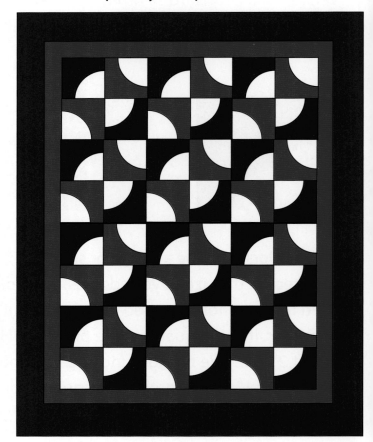

Quilt Layout

Totes Galore
Approximate Size: 24" x 44"

If you have collected lots of totes at quilt shows or other special occasions, you might now have boxes filled with them. Why not make a wall hanging that uses the totes as pockets to hold those little items you will now need to make your upcycle quilts.

Materials

6 canvas tote bags (at least 10½" x 10½" each)

¾ yd lt blue cotton twill

1 yd dk blue cotton twill

1½ yds backing fabric

batting

Cutting

*6 squares, 10½" x 10½", Totes

6 rectangles, 9½" x 12½", dk blue twill

3 strips, 2½" x 12½", lt blue twill (sashing)

2 strips, 2½" x 20½", lt blue twill (sashing)

2 strips, 2½" x 40½", lt blue twill (border)

2 strips, 2½" x 24½", lt blue twill (border)

4 strips, 2½"-wide, lt blue twill (binding)

*When cutting squares from totes, do not cut top hemmed edge.

Tips for Using Tote Bags

• Pick tote bags of similar thickness for your wall hanging.

• Use thicker fabric such as a cotton twill for the background since the tote bags are most often canvas or heavy-weight muslin.

• Remove handles and cut side seams from each tote bag.

Instructions

Making the Blocks

1. About 2" from each side, make a ½" pleat in lower edge of tote square; pin or baste pleats in place. **Note:** *The pleated lower edge should measure 9½".*

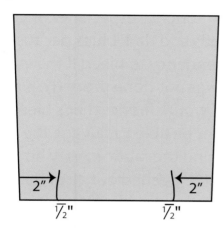

2. Place tote square right side up on right side of dk blue twill rectangle, lining up lower edges. Sew along the sides and lower edge with a scant ¼" seam allowance.

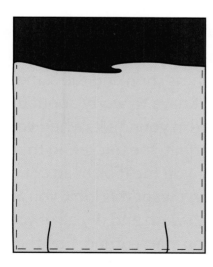

3. Repeat steps 1 and 2 for remaining five blocks.

Finishing your Wall Tote

1. Referring to Quilt Layout, place tote blocks in a pleasing arrangement in three rows of two blocks with a 2½" x 12½" lt blue twill sashing strip in between.

2. Sew rows of blocks together with a 2½" x 20½" lt blue twill sashing strip in between.

3. Refer to Adding Borders, pages 57 to 59, to add lt blue twill border.

4. Refer to Finishing Your Quilt, pages 60 to 64, to complete your Totes wall hanging.

Quilt Layout

General Directions

Fabric

For over a hundred years, quilts have been made with 100% cotton fabric, the choice for most quilters.

There are many properties in cotton that make it especially well-suited to quilt making. There is less distortion in cotton fabric, thereby affording the quilter greater security in making certain that even the smallest bits of fabric will fit together. Because a quilt block made of cotton can be ironed flat with a steam iron, a puckered area, created by mistake, can be fixed. The sewing machine needle can move through cotton with a great deal of ease when compared to some synthetic fabrics. While you may find that quilt artists today often use other kinds of fabric, to create the quilts quickly and accurately, 100% cotton is strongly recommended.

Cotton fabric today is produced in so many wonderful and exciting combinations of prints and solids that it is often difficult to pick colors for your quilt. We've chosen our favorite colors for these quilts, but don't be afraid to make your own choices.

For years, quilters were advised to prewash all of their fabric to test for colorfastness and shrinkage. Now most quilters don't bother to prewash all of their fabric but they do pretest it. Cut a strip about 2" wide from each piece of fabric that you will use in your quilt. Measure both the length and the width of the strip. Then immerse it in a bowl of very hot water, using a separate bowl for each piece of fabric. Be especially concerned about reds and dark blues because they have a tendency to bleed if the initial dyeing was not done properly. If it's one of your favorite fabrics that's bleeding, you might be able to salvage the fabric. Try washing the fabric in very hot water until you've washed out all of the excess dye. Unfortunately, fabrics that continue to bleed after they have been washed repeatedly will bleed forever. So eliminate them right at the start.

Now, take each one of the strips and iron them dry with a hot iron. Be especially careful not to stretch the strip. When the strips are completely dry, measure and compare them to your original strip. If all of your fabric is shrinking the same amount, you don't have to worry about uneven shrinkage in your quilt. When you wash the final quilt, the puckering that will result may give you the look of an antique quilt. If you don't want this look, you are going to have to wash and dry all of your fabric before you start cutting. Iron the fabric using some spray starch or sizing to give fabric a crisp finish.

If you are never planning to wash your quilt, i.e. your quilt is intended to be a wall hanging such as many of the quilts in this collection, you could eliminate the pre-testing process. You may run the risk, however, of some future relative to whom you have willed your quilts deciding that the wall hanging needs freshening by washing.

Before beginning to work, make sure that your fabric is absolutely square. If it is not, you will have difficulty cutting square pieces. Fabric is woven with crosswise and lengthwise threads. Lengthwise threads should be parallel to the selvage (that's the finished edge along the sides; sometimes the fabric company prints its name along the selvage), and crosswise threads should be perpendicular to the selvage. If fabric is off grain, you can usually straighten it by pulling gently on the true bias in the opposite direction to the off-grain edge. Continue doing this until the crosswise threads are at a right angle to the lengthwise threads.

Rotary Cutting

Supplies for Rotary Cutting

For rotary cutting, you will need three important tools: a rotary cutter, a mat and an acrylic ruler. There are currently on the market many different brands and types. Choose the kinds that you feel will work for you. Ask your quilting friends what their preferences are, then make your decision.

There are several different rotary cutters now available with special features that you might prefer such as the type of handle, whether the cutter can be used for both right- and left-handed quilters, safety features, size, and finally the cost.

Don't attempt to use the rotary cutter without an accompanying protective mat. The mat will not only protect your table from becoming scratched, but it will protect your cutter as well. The mat is self-healing and will not dull the cutting blades. Mats are available in many sizes, but if this is your first attempt at rotary cutting, an 18" x 24" mat is probably your best choice. When you are not using your mat, be sure to store it on a flat surface. Otherwise your mat will bend. If you want to keep your mat from warping, make certain that it is not sitting in direct sunlight; the heat can cause the mat to warp. You will not be able to cut accurately when you use a bent or warped mat.

Another must for cutting accurate strips is a strong straight edge. Acrylic rulers are the perfect choice for this. There are many different brands of acrylic rulers on the market, and they come in several widths and lengths. Either a 6" x 24" or a 6" x 12" ruler will be the most useful. The longer ruler will allow you to fold your fabric only once while the smaller size will require folding the fabric twice. Make sure that your ruler has $\frac{1}{8}$" increment markings in both directions plus a 45-degree marking.

Cutting Strips With a Rotary Cutter

Before beginning to work, iron your fabric to remove the wrinkles. Fold the fabric in half, lengthwise, bringing the selvage edges together. Fold in half again. Make sure that there are no wrinkles in the fabric.

Now place the folded fabric on the cutting mat. Place the fabric length on the right side if you are right-handed or on the left side if you are left-handed. The fold of the fabric should line up along one of the grid lines printed on the mat. **(Diagram 1)**

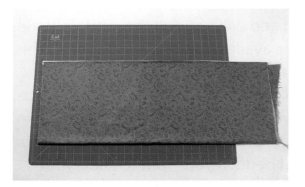

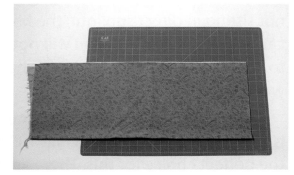

Straighten one of the cut edges first. **(Diagram 2)**

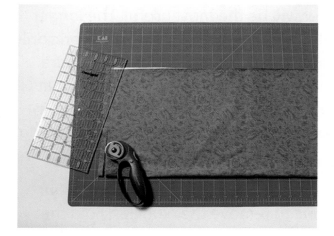

Lay the acrylic ruler on the mat near the cut edge; the ruler markings should be even with the grid on the mat. Hold the ruler firmly with your left hand (or, with your right hand if you are left-handed). To provide extra stability, keep your small finger off the mat. Now hold the rotary cutter with blade against the ruler and cut away from you in one quick motion.

Carefully turn the fabric (or mat with the fabric) so the straightened edge is on the opposite side. Place the ruler on the required width line along the cut edge of the fabric and cut the strip, making sure that you always cut away from you — never toward you. Cut the number of strips called for in the directions. **(Diagram 3)**

After you have cut a few strips, you will want to check to make certain that your fabric continues to be perfectly square. To do this, just line up the crosswise markings along the folded edge of fabric and the lengthwise edge of the ruler next to the end of fabric you are cutting. Cut off uneven edge. If you fail to do this, your strips may be bowed with a "v" in the center, causing your piecing to become inaccurate as you continue working.

Cutting Squares and Rectangles

Now that you have cut your strips, you can begin to cut squares or rectangles. Place a stack of strips on the cutting mat. You will be more successful in cutting — at least in the beginning — if you work with no more than four strips at a time. Make certain that the strips are lined up very evenly. Following the instructions given for the quilt, cut the required number of squares or rectangles. **(Diagram 4)**

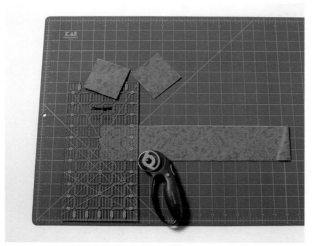

Cutting Triangles

Once your squares are cut, you can cut triangles, including half-square triangles and triangle squares.

Half-Square Triangles

The short sides of a half-square triangle are on the short grain of the fabric. This is especially necessary if the short edges are on the outer side of the block.

Cut the squares the size indicated in the instructions, then cut the square in half diagonally. **(Diagram 5)**

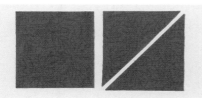

Triangle Squares

These are squares made up of two different-colored triangles. To make these squares, you can cut individual triangles as described in Half-Square Triangles above. Then sew two triangles together. A quick method, especially if you have several triangle squares with the same fabric, is to sew two squares together. Then draw a diagonal line on the wrong side of the lighter square. Place two squares right sides together and sew ¼" from each side of the drawn line.

Cut along the drawn line, and you have created two triangle squares. **(Diagram 6)**

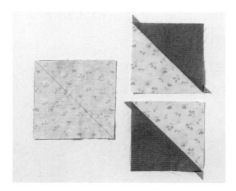

Stitch and Flip

This is a method for quickly creating triangles and octagons or trapezoids.

Instead of cutting these shapes, cut and sew squares or rectangles together. **(Diagram 7)**

With right sides together, place a small square in the corner of a larger square or rectangle. Then sew diagonally from corner to corner of the small square. **(Diagram 8)**

Trim the corner about ¼" from the seam line. **(Diagram 9).**

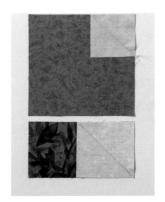

Flip the triangle over and iron. **(Diagram 10)**

Repeat at the other corners. (**Diagram 11)**

Strip Piecing

Strip piecing is a much faster and easier method of making quilts rather than creating the blocks piece by piece. With this method, two or more strips are sewn together and then cut at certain intervals.

For instance, if a block is made up of several 3" finished squares, cut 3½"-wide strips along the crosswise grain. **(Diagram 12)**

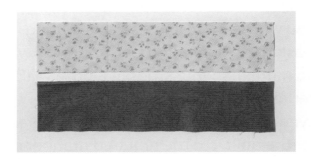

With right sides together, sew two strips along the length. The seam should be pressed to the dark side of the fabric. **(Diagram 13)**

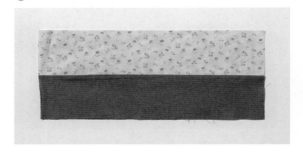

Cut across strips at 3½" intervals to create pairs of 3½" squares. **(Diagram 14)**

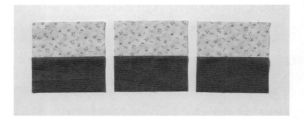

Foundation Piecing

Materials

Before you begin, decide the kind of foundation on which you are planning to piece the blocks.

Paper

The most popular choice is paper. It's readily available and fairly inexpensive. You can use copy paper, newsprint, tracing paper - even computer paper. The paper does not remain a permanent part of your quilt as it is removed once the blocks are completely sewn.

Fabric

If you choose to hand piece your block, you may want to choose fabric as your foundation. Just remember that fabric is not removed after you make your block so you will have another layer to quilt through. This may be a problem if you are planning to hand quilt. Using fabric might be an advantage, however, if you want to use some non-traditional quilting fabrics, such as silk or satin, since the fabric foundation will add stability to the block. Fabric makes a good choice for crazy quilts. If you do decide to use fabric, choose a lightweight and light-colored fabric, such as muslin, that will allow you to see through for ease in tracing.

Other Materials

Another option for foundation materials is Tear Away™ or Fun-dation™, translucent non-woven materials combining both the advantages of both paper and fabric. They are easy to see through, but like paper they can be removed with ease.

Currently a new kind of foundation material has appeared in the market place: a foundation paper that dissolves in water after use. Two companies, W.H. Collins and EZ Quilting by Wrights are producing this product.

Preparing the Foundation

Place your foundation material over your chosen block and trace the block pattern. Use a ruler and a fine-line pencil or permanent marker, and make sure that all lines are straight. Sometimes short dashed lines or even dotted lines are easier to make. Be sure to copy all numbers. You will need to make a foundation for each block you are planning to use.

If you have a home copier, you can copy your tracing on the copy machine. Since the copy machine might slightly alter the measurements of the block, make certain that you copy each block from the original pattern.

You can also scan the block if you have a home scanner and then print out the required number of blocks.

Cutting the Fabric

In foundation piecing, you do not have to cut perfect shapes!

You can, therefore, use odd pieces of fabric: squares, strips, rectangles. The one thing you must remember, however, is that every piece must be at least ¼" larger on all sides than the space it is going to cover. Strips and squares are easy: just measure the length and width of the needed space and add ½" all around. Cut your strip to that measurement. Triangles, however, can be a bit tricky. In that case, measure the widest point of the triangle and cut your fabric about ½" to 1" wider.

Other Supplies for Foundation Piecing

Piecing by hand:

You will need a reasonably thin needle such as a Sharp size 10; a good-quality, neutral-colored thread such as a size 50 cotton; some pins, a glue stick; fabric scissors; muslin or fabric for the bases.

Piecing by machine:

You will need a cleaned and oiled sewing machine; glue stick; pins, paper scissors, fabric scissors, foundation material.

Before beginning to sew your actual block by machine, determine the proper stitch length. Use a piece of the paper you are planning to use for the foundation and draw a straight line on it. Set your machine so that it sews with a fairly short stitch (about 20 stitches per inch). Sew along the line. If you can tear the paper apart with ease, you are sewing with the right length. You don't want to sew with such a short stitch that the paper falls apart by itself. If you are going to use a fabric foundation with the sewing machine, use the stitch length you normally use since you won't be removing the fabric foundation.

Using a Pattern

The numbers on the block show the order in which the pieces are to be placed and sewn on the base.

It is extremely important that you follow the numbers; otherwise the entire process won't work.

Making the Blocks

The important thing to remember about making a foundation block is that the fabric pieces go on the unmarked side of the foundation while you sew on the printed side. The finished blocks are a mirror image of the original pattern.

Step 1: Hold the foundation up to a light source - even a window pane - with the unmarked side facing. Find the space marked 1 on the unmarked side and put a dab of glue there. Place the fabric right side up on the unmarked side on Space 1, making certain that the fabric overlaps at least ¼" on all sides of space 1. **(Diagram 15)**

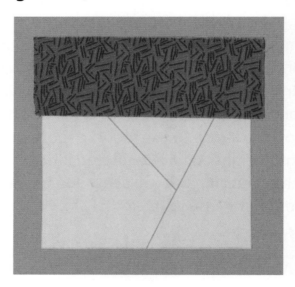

Step 2: Fold the foundation along the line between Space 1 and Space 2. Cut the fabric so that it is ¼" from the fold. **(Diagram 16)**

Step 3: With right sides together, place Fabric Piece 2 on Fabric Piece 1, making sure that the edge of Piece 2 is even with the just-trimmed edge of Piece 1. **(Diagram 17)**

Step 4: To make certain that Piece 2 will cover Space 2, fold the fabric piece back along the line between Space 1 and Space 2. **(Diagram 18)**

Step 5: With the marked side of the foundation facing up, place the piece on the sewing machine (or sew by hand), holding both Piece 1 and Piece 2 in place. Sew along the line between Space 1 and Space 2. **(Diagram 19)**

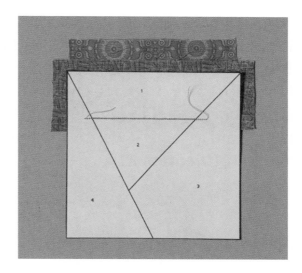

If you use a small stitch, it will be easier to remove the paper later. Start sewing about two or three stitches before the beginning of the line and end your sewing two or three stitches beyond the line. This will allow the stitching to be held in place by the next round of stitching rather than by backstitching.

Step 6: Turn the work over and open Piece 2. Finger press the seam open. **(Diagram 20)**

Step 7: Turning the work so that the marked side is on top, fold the foundation forward along the line between Space 1+2 and Space 3. Trim about ⅛" to ¼" from the fold. It is easier to trim the paper if you pull the paper away from the stitching. If you use fabric as your foundation, fold the fabric forward as far as it will go and then start to trim. **(Diagram 21)**

Step 8: Place Fabric #3 right side down even with the just-trimmed edge. **(Diagram 22)**

Step 9: Turn the block over to the marked side and sew along the line between Space 1+2 and Space 3. **(Diagram 23)**

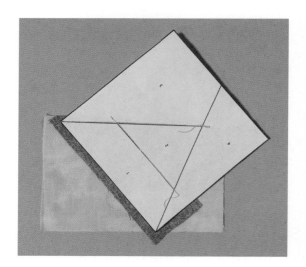

Step 10: Turn the work over, open Piece 3 and finger press the seam. **(Diagram 24)**

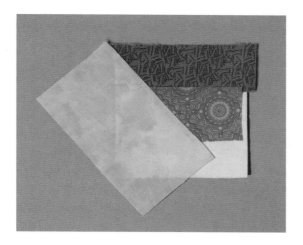

Step 11: In the same way you have added the other pieces, add Piece #4 to complete this block. Trim the fabric ¼" from the edge of the foundation. The foundation-pieced block is completed. **(Diagram 25)**

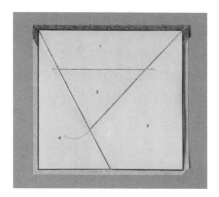

After you have finished sewing a block, don't immediately remove the paper. Since you are often piecing with tiny bits of fabric, grainline is never a factor. Therefore, some of the pieces may have been cut on the bias and may have a tendency to stretch. You can eliminate any problem with distortion by keeping the paper in place until all of the blocks have been sewn together. If, however, you want to remove the paper, stay stitch along the outer edge of the block to help keep the block in shape.

Sewing Multiple Sections

Some blocks in foundation piecing are created with two or more sections. These sections, which are indicated by letters, are individually pieced and then sewn together. The cutting line for these sections is indicated by a bold line. Before you start to make any of these multi-section blocks, begin by cutting the foundation piece apart so that each section is worked independently. Leave a ¼" seam allowance around each section.

Step 1: Following the instructions above for Making the Block, complete each section. Then place the sections right side together. Pin the corners of the top section to the corners of the bottom section. **(Diagram 26)**

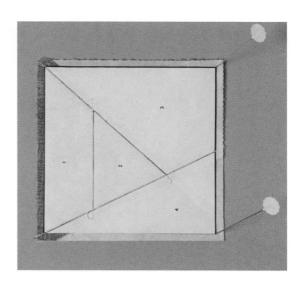

Step 2: If you are certain that the pieces are aligned correctly, sew the two sections together using the regular stitch length on the sewing machine.
(Diagram 27)

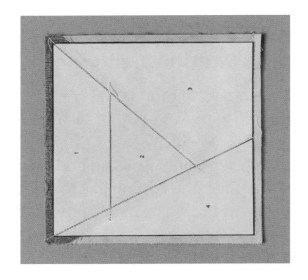

Step 3: Press the sections open and continue sewing the sections in pairs.
(Diagram 28)

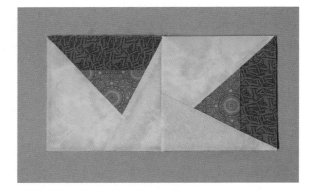

Step 4: Sew necessary pairs of sections together to complete the block.
(Diagram 29)

The blocks are now ready to sew into your quilts.

What You Don't Want to Forget

1. If you plan to sew by hand, begin by taking some backstitches which will anchor the thread at the beginning of the line. Then use a backstitch every four or five stitches. End the stitching with a few backstitches.

2. If you plan to sew by machine, start stitching two or three stitches before the start of the stitching line and finish your stitching two or three stitches beyond the end.

3. Use a short stitch (about 20 stitches per inch) for paper foundations to make it easier to remove the paper. If the paper falls apart as you sew, your stitches are too short.

4. Finger press (or use an iron) each seam as you finish it.

5. Stitching which goes from a space into another space will not interfere with adding additional fabric pieces.

6. Remember to trim all seam allowances at least ¼".

7. When sewing points, start from the wide end and sew towards the point.

8. Unless you plan to use it only once in the block, it is a good idea to stay away from directional prints in foundation piecing.

9. When cutting pieces for foundation piecing, never worry about the grainline.

10. Always remember to sew on the marked side, placing the fabric on the unmarked side.

11. Follow the numerical order, or it won't work.

12. Once you have finished making a block, do not remove the paper until the entire quilt has been finished unless you stay stitch around the outside of the block.

13. Be sure that the ink you use to make your foundation is permanent and will not wash out into your fabric.

Making a Quilt

Sewing the Blocks Together

Once all of the blocks for your quilt have been made, place them on a flat surface

such as a design wall or floor to decide on the best placement.

Sew the blocks together. You can do this by sewing the blocks in rows, then sewing the rows together; or, sew the blocks in pairs then sew pairs together. Continue

sewing in pairs until entire quilt top is sewn together. **(Diagram 30)**

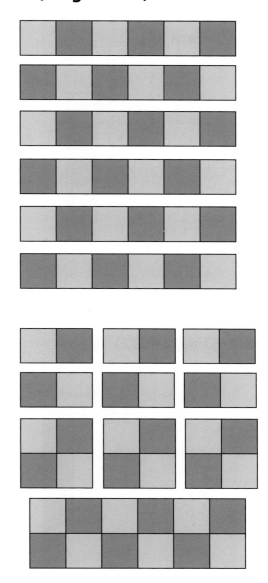

Adding Borders

Borders are usually added to a quilt sides first, then top and bottom.

Simple Borders

Step 1: Measure the quilt top lengthwise and cut two border strips to that length by the width measurement given in the project instructions. Strips may have to be pieced to achieve the correct length. To make the joining seam less noticeable, sew the strips together diagonally. Place two strips right sides together at right angles. Sew a diagonal seam. **(Diagram 31)**

Step 2: Trim excess fabric ¼" from stitching. **(Diagram 32)**

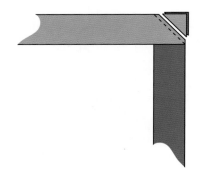

Step 3: Press seam open. **(Diagram 33)**

Step 4: Sew strips to the sides of the quilt. Now measure the quilt top crosswise, being sure to include the borders you have just added. Cut two border strips, following the width measurement given in the instructions.

Step 5: Add these borders to the top and bottom of the quilt. Repeat this process for any additional borders. Use the ¼" seam allowance at all times and press all of the seams to the darker side. Press the quilt top carefully.

Mitered Borders

Mitered borders are much more time-consuming, but sometimes the results may well be worth the effort.

Step 1: Measure the quilt top lengthwise. Cut two strips that length plus twice the finished border width plus ½" for seam allowances. Piece if necessary, referring to Step 1 in Simple Borders above.

Step 2: Measure the quilt top crosswise. Cut, piecing if necessary, two strips that length plus twice the finished border width plus ½".

Step 3: Find the midpoint of border strip by folding strip in half. **(Diagram 34)**

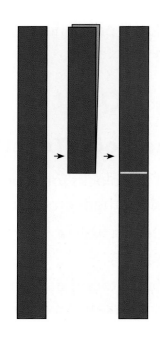

Step 4: Place strip right sides together with quilt top matching midpoint of border with midpoint of quilt side. Pin in place. **(Diagram 35)**

Pin border to quilt top along entire side.

Step 5: Beginning ¼" from top edge, sew border strip to quilt top, ending ¼" from bottom edge. Backstitch at beginning and ending of sewing. **(Diagram 36)**

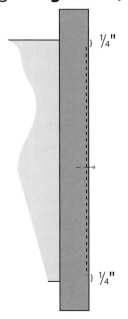

Step 6: To finish corners, fold quilt top in half diagonally right sides together; borders will extend straight up and away from quilt. Place ruler along folded edge of quilt top going into border strip; draw a diagonal line on the border. **(Diagram 37)**

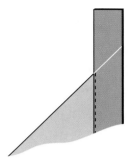

Step 7: Beginning at corner of quilt top, stitch along drawn line to edge of border strip. **(Diagram 38)**

Step 8: Open quilt at corner to check miter. If satisfied, trim excess fabric ¼" from diagonal seam. **(Diagram 39)**

Step 9: Repeat process on remaining three corners.

Finishing Your Quilt

Attaching the Batting and Backing

There are a number of different types of batting on the market today including the new fusible battings that eliminate the need for basting. Your choice of batting will depend upon how you are planning to use your quilt. If the quilt is to serve as a wall hanging, you will probably want to use a thin cotton batting. A quilt made with a thin cotton or cotton/polyester blend works best for machine quilting. Very thick polyester batting should be used only for tied quilts.

The best fabric for quilt backing is 100% cotton fabric. If your quilt is larger than the available fabric, you will have to piece your backing fabric. When joining the fabric, try not to have a seam going down the center. Instead cut off the selvages and make a center strip that is about 36" wide and have narrower strips at the sides. Seam the pieces together and carefully iron the seams open. (This is one of the few times in making a quilt that a seam should be pressed open.) Several fabric manufacturers are now selling fabric in 90"or 108"-widths for use as backing fabric.

It is a good idea to remove the batting from its wrapping 24 hours before you plan to use it and open it out to full size. You will find that the batting will now lie flat when you are ready to use it.

The batting and the backing should be cut about one to two inches larger on all sides than the quilt top. Place the backing wrong side up on a flat surface. Smooth out the batting on top of this, matching the outer edges. Center the quilt top, right side up, on top of the batting.

Now the quilt layers must be held together before quilting, and there are several methods for doing this:

Safety-pin Basting: Starting from the center and working toward the edges, pin through all layers at one time with large safety pins. The pins should be placed no more than 4" apart. As you work, think of your quilting plan to make sure that the pins will avoid prospective quilting lines.

Thread Basting: Baste the three layers together with long stitches. Start in the center and sew toward the edges in a number of diagonal lines.

Quilt-gun Basting: This handy trigger tool pushes nylon tags through all layers of the quilt. Start in the center and work toward the outside edges. The tags should be placed about 4" apart. You can sew right over the tags, which can then be easily removed by cutting them off with scissors.

Spray or Heat-Set Basting: Several manufacturers have spray adhesives available especially for quilters. Apply these products by following the manufacturers' directions. You might want to test these products before you use them to make sure that they meet your requirements.

Fusible Iron-on Batting: These battings are a wonderful new way to hold quilt layers together without using any of the other time-consuming methods of basting. Again, you will want to test these battings to be certain that you are happy with the results. Follow the manufacturers' directions.

Quilting

If you like the process of hand quilting, you can–of course–finish these projects by hand quilting. However, if you want to finish these quilts quickly, in the time we are suggesting, you will want to use a sewing machine for quilting.

If you have never used a sewing machine for quilting, you may want to find a book and read about the technique. You do not need a special machine for quilting. Just make sure that your machine has been oiled and is in good working condition.

If you are going to do machine quilting, you should invest in an even-feed foot. This foot is designed to feed the top and bottom layers of a quilt evenly through the machine. The foot prevents puckers from forming as you machine quilt. Use a fine transparent nylon thread in the top and regular sewing thread in the bobbin.

Quilting in the ditch is one of the easiest ways to machine quilt.

This is a term used to describe stitching along the seam line between two pieces of fabric. Using your fingers, pull the blocks or pieces apart slightly and machine stitch right between the two pieces. The stitching will look better if you keep the stitching to the side of the seam that does not have the extra bulk of the seam allowance under it. The quilting will be hidden in the seam.

Free-form machine quilting can be used to quilt around a design or to quilt a motif. The quilting is done with a darning foot and the feed dogs down on the sewing machine. It takes practice to master Free-form quilting because you are controlling the movement of the quilt under the needle rather than the sewing machine moving the quilt. You can quilt in any direction—up and down, side-to-side and even in circles—without pivoting the quilt around the needle. Practice this quilting method before trying it on your quilt.

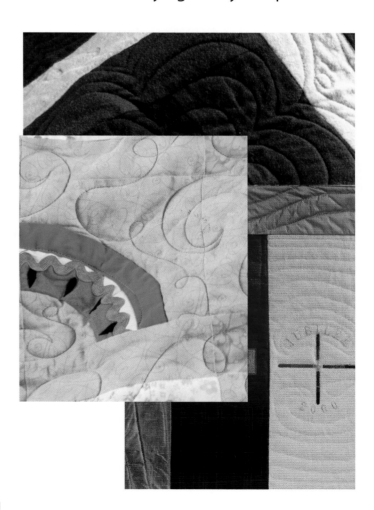

Attaching the Continuous Machine Binding

Once the quilt has been quilted, it must be bound to cover the raw edges.

Step 1: Start by trimming the backing and batting even with the quilt top. Measure the quilt top and cut enough 2½" wide strips to go around all four sides of the quilt plus 12". Join the strips end to end with diagonal seams and trim the corners. **(Diagram 40)** Press the seams open.

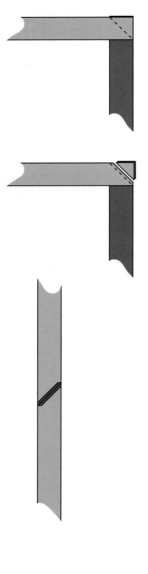

Step 2: Cut one end of the strip at a 45-degree angle and press under ¼". **(Diagram 41)**

Step 3: Press entire strip in half lengthwise, wrong sides together. **(Diagram 42)**

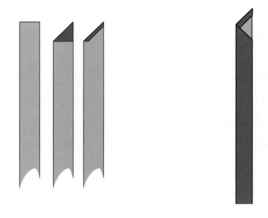

Step 4: On the back of the quilt, position the binding in the middle of one side, keeping the raw edges together. Sew the binding to the quilt with the ¼" seam allowance, beginning about three inches below the folded end of the binding. **(Diagram 43)**

At the corner, stop ¼" from the edge of the quilt and backstitch.

Step 5: Fold binding away from quilt so it is at a right angle to edge just sewn. Then, fold the binding back on itself so the fold is on the quilt edge and the raw edges are aligned with the adjacent side of the quilt. Begin sewing at the quilt edge. **(Diagram 44)**

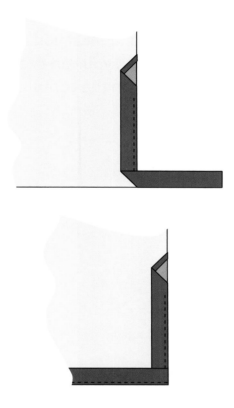

Step 6: Continue in the same way around the remaining sides of the quilt. Stop about 2" away from the starting point. Trim any excess binding and tuck it inside the folded end. Finish the stitching.

(Diagram 45)

Step 7: Fold the binding to the front of the quilt so the seam line is covered; machine-stitch the binding in place on the front of the quilt. Use a straight stitch or tiny zigzag with invisible or matching thread. If you have a sewing machine that does embroidery stitches, you may want to use your favorite stitch.

Adding a Rod Pocket

In order to hang your quilt for family and friends to enjoy, you will need to attach a rod pocket to the back.

Step 1: Cut a strip of fabric, 6" wide by the width of the quilt.

Step 2: Fold short ends of strip under ¼", then fold another ¼". Sew along first fold. **(Diagram 46)**

Step 3: Fold strip lengthwise with wrong sides together. Sew along raw edges with a ¼" seam allowance to form a long tube. **(Diagram 47)**

Step 4: Place tube on ironing surface with seam up and centered; press seam open and fold flat. **(Diagram 48)**

Step 5: Place tube on back of quilt, seam side against quilt, about 1" from top edge and equal distance from side edges. **(Diagram 49)**

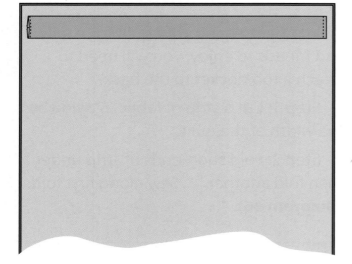

Pin in place so tube is straight across quilt.

Step 6: Hand stitch top and bottom edges of tube to back of quilt being careful not to let stitches show on front of quilt.

Labeling Your Quilt

Always sign and date your quilt when finished. You can make a label by cross-stitching or embroidering or even writing on a label with a permanent marking pen on the back of your quilt. If you are friends with your computer, you can even create an attractive label on the computer.